WILD CAMPING IN SCOTLAND

JAMES CARRON

Amenta Publishing

www.amenta.ink

WILD CAMPING IN SCOTLAND

ISBN: 9781097848294

First published 2013 by Amenta Publishing

Second, revised edition published 2020

Copyright © James Carron 2020

The right of James Carron to be identified as the author of this work has been asserted by him in accordance with the Copyright, Designs and Patents Act 1988.

All rights reserved. No part of this publication may be reproduced, stored in a retrieval system, or transmitted in any form, or by any means, electronic, mechanical, photocopying, recording or otherwise, without permission in writing from the publisher.

Disclaimer: Every effort has been made to ensure that the information in this book is correct at the time of publication. Walking and wild camping can be dangerous and is done entirely at your own risk. The author and publisher can accept no responsibility for any accident or injury sustained while following the information provided in this guide. We strongly recommend the use of appropriate Ordnance Survey or similar mapping when exploring the countryside. If you encounter any changes on the ground, please email jimcarron@gmail.com and we will investigate and update the text as necessary.

CONTENTS

Introduction	4
A Brief History of Wild Camping	6
Wild Camping Kit	9
Pick a Pitch	20
Legal Stuff	33
The Sites	43

INTRODUCTION

Scotland has a rich tradition of wild camping. It has long been an accepted part of the outdoor scene with campers enjoying the freedom to pitch up in quite corners of the countryside. In 2003, it was recognised by the Land Reform (Scotland) Act which, for the first time, established a legal right to camp on just about any land.

Wild camping is one of the best ways to enjoy the tranquillity and scenic splendour of the nation's mountains, glens and coastal areas and can be undertaken as an activity in its own right or combined with pursuits such as cycling, hillwalking or canoeing.

With no facilities to hand, the freedom to pitch up miles from anywhere and enjoy uninterrupted views across open countryside more than compensates. Divest of the shackles of civilisation, there really is no better way to spend a few peaceful nights out.

CAMPING ON THE ISLE OF RUM

A skill in its own right, the key to successful wild camping is to be as unobtrusive as possible, to aim for minimal impact on the landscape and the wildlife that inhabits it and to leave no trace of your having been there, other than some flattened blades of grass.

This book offers a guide to wild camping in Scotland. At its heart is a listing of 25 'perfect pitches', a handpicked selection of exceptional sites for wild camping in the Scottish Highlands and Islands. Each is described and illustrated and accompanied by fact file information to enable readers to visit and pitch up for themselves. Sites range from easily accessible spots, suitable for novice wild campers or families, to wilder, more remote locations, accessible only on foot, by bike or across the water.

Complementing this is advice on how to get the best out of a wild camping trip and information on useful equipment and kit. There is also a guide to the law covering the countryside and an overview of the Scottish Outdoor Access Code.

PITCHED BY THE DAVA WAY, ABERDEENSHIRE

A BRIEF HISTORY OF WILD CAMPING

Wild Camping has been practised in Scotland in one form or another for centuries. In the early years, the increasing popularity of the Breacan an Fhéilidh or Féileadh Mor (great kilt) allowed Scotsmen to sleep out on the moors without need for any additional shelter.

Measuring up to 16 feet in length and over four feet in width, the thick untailored woollen cloth was traditionally worn with a wide belt at the waist. With plenty of material to spare, it doubled up as both a ground sheet and sleeping bag, creating an early form of bivvy bag. Generations of clansmen, moving through the mountains and glens, lived in their kilts. It was a practice well used by both legitimate cattle drovers walking stock from the Highlands and Islands to markets in central and southern Scotland and their archenemies, the cattle rustlers.

In the 18th century, droving inns, and later hotels, began to spring up on popular routes. However, the writings of 19th century travellers like Dorothy Wordsworth suggest many were rather basic and often insalubrious establishments. She described one of Scotland's oldest licensed inns, the King's House Hotel, in Glencoe, as a 'wretched' place.

'Never did I see such a miserable, such a wretched place – long rooms with ranges of beds, no other furniture except benches, or perhaps one or two crazy chairs, the floors far dirtier than an ordinary house could be if it were never washed,' was her view of the establishment.

'With length of time the fire was kindled and after another hour of waiting, supper came, a shoulder of mutton so hard that it was impossible to chew the little flesh that might have been scraped off the bones.'

With reviews of this type common, the practice of sleeping out continued.

GATHERING ROUND A CAMPFIRE IN THE CAIRNGORMS

It was the 1920s and 30s before wild camping became a popular recreational pursuit. Between the two great wars, Scotland saw a boom in hillwalking and mountaineering with more and more people escaping the urban sprawl for weekends in the countryside. Unable to afford hotels and with youth hostels yet to be established, they found shelter where they could. Some camped in canvas or cotton tents while others stayed in informal natural shelters, such as caves and howffs, or in barns, abandoned shepherds' cottages or bothies.

At the time the law regarding wild camping was unclear. The Trespass (Scotland) Act 1865 technically made it an offence to camp on land without the consent of the owner. While some landowners tolerated the practice (and some campers sought permission before pitching), others were vehemently opposed and 'no camping' signs started to spring up.

It was not until the Land Reform (Scotland) Act 2003 came into effect in 2005 that the legal position was clarified. Under the new legislation, responsible wild camping was included in the list of activities for which access rights applied.

In short, wild camping is camping on land out with formal campsites. The Land Reform (Scotland) Act 2003 allows camping on any land where access rights apply. The land does not have to be particularly 'wild' or remote and wild camping is not restricted to so called wilderness areas.

GROUP CAMPING

WILD CAMPING KIT

TENTS

There are a number of factors to consider when picking the best tent for a wild camping trip. Smaller tents with a lower profile are better than large family-style ones. They are lighter to carry and less conspicuous, reducing impact on the landscape. In rougher countryside, it tends to be easier to find flat spots of ground for small tents so if there are several people in the party, opt for two or more wee ones rather than one big one. Small tents are also easier to pitch in wet and windy weather.

Select an A-frame, dome, tunnel or geodesic shape, all of which offer wind resistance, rigidity and stability.

Tunnel tents offer good internal space and generous headroom. They are also quick and easy to pitch. However, they tend to be less stable and care must be taken to pitch either front or rear end into the prevailing wind (not always easy in Scotland's changeable climate). It is always best to fully guy out a tunnel tent, regardless of the conditions.

TUNNEL TENT

A SIMPLE DOME TENT

Semi geodesic tents – where the poles cross over each other to create a dome shape – are much more stable but they are heavier and more complex to erect. Designs vary, as do pole numbers and configurations. As a general rule, a tent is considered to be semi geodesic when the poles cross at between two and four points.

Fully geodesic tents are extremely stable. Again they are heavier and more complex to erect and they are expensive but they will withstand all but the most severe weather conditions. Poles cross at five or more points, creating a very rigid and unyielding structure.

Dome tents are a useful compromise between tunnel and geodesic, offering a high level of stability coupled with straightforward pitching and low weight. In a dome tent, the main poles cross each other only once, at the highest point.

INNER OR OUTER FIRST?

When it comes to pitching there are two basic differences in tent design – some go up inner first while others are erected flysheet first. On a tent that pitches inner first, the poles are threaded through or clipped to the inner first, the ground sheet is pegged out and then the flysheet is

FULLY GEODESIC EXPEDITION TENT

attached over the top. This type of tent tends to be more streamlined and more stable as the fly and inner are tensioned together. However, in bad weather, the inner is exposed to the elements during pitching in the rain and it may be tricky to get the flysheet on if it is windy. They cannot be pitched as a single unit and are often less well ventilated.

On a tent that pitches outer first, the poles are threaded through or clipped to the flysheet, which is the initial section to go up. The inner is then clipped inside. The inner and outer can also be left together and pitched as one. This type of tent is slightly less streamlined but the inner does remain dry when striking camp in the wet.

SIZE

A significant factor to consider when choosing a tent is the number of people in the party. For a solo expedition either a lightweight one-person tent or bivvy bag are ideal, although the latter severely restricts space available to stow gear or cook under cover. For two or more people, two or three-person tents will be required and the weight can be shared.

Tent selection is always a compromise between what you are prepared to carry and how comfortable you want to be. For a night or two you might be able to put up with cramped conditions while on longer forays, a little more space to manoeuvre and some headroom might be appreciated.

It is also worth bearing in mind that when wild camping in remote spots sloping off to the pub, a café or hotel is not usually an option and if the weather is bad you may spend significant amounts of time confined to the tent.

Carefully consider how much space you need to sleep comfortably and stow kit. A porch is useful not only for keeping boots and wet gear out of the inner tent but also for cooking in bad weather or when there are midges about.

LIGHTWEIGHT BACKPACKING TUNNEL TENT

BUDGET

The cost of tents varies greatly. It is possible to pick up a cheap but perfectly usable two-person one for between £20 and £50. If you are camping on low ground in the summer, fairly close to civilisation, this is all you really need, especially if the trip is a one-off or taster. Discount outdoor stores, supermarkets and catalogue shops are good sources of inexpensive tents but expect some shortcomings. The fabric – the ground sheet in particular – might not be particularly hardwearing. The design may not be very robust. There might be very limited storage space or no porch for cooking. The overall package may be heavy. Avoid cheap pop-up tents designed for festivals as they are less stable and offer fewer features.

Move up to the £100 to £200 bracket and you will find a much greater selection of designs, more features and lighter models.

A-FRAME TENT

COLOUR

Wild campers seeking minimal impact should opt for tents that blend into the landscape. Greens, browns and blacks are less noticeable than brightly coloured or patterned tents designed with festivalgoers in mind.

PITCHING AND PACKING

If you are taking a brand new tent on its first outing (or are borrowing one from a friend), always pitch it in the garden at home or a local park before you set off and make sure all the bits are there. The last thing you want to do is reach a distant spot only to find that a vital component is missing.

When packing a tent in a rucksack, split the various parts rather than simply lump the whole lot in together. This will distribute the weight more evenly. Poles can either be pushed down the side of the sack or attached to the outside. Pegs can go in a pocket while the inner tent and flysheet should go in the main body of the sack, close to the top. The key is to ensure everything is easily accessible so you do not have to empty the whole sack to get the tent out. This will pay dividends if you have to pitch in bad weather.

Once pitched, always zip up the inner door when you are out of the tent (even for a short time) to prevent insects getting in.

Condensation is an issue most campers will experience. To minimise this, ensure all available vents are open, keep storm flaps rolled up unless needed and shake off or wipe away any moisture that gathers under the flysheet.

TENT CARE

Moisture and dirt are a tent's greatest enemies and, camping in Scotland, both are unavoidable, which means time must be spent on cleaning and drying, something that is particularly important before a tent is stored for any length of time.

Out on an expedition, if your tent does get wet while pitched, take advantage of any spells of good weather to let it dry out naturally before taking it down.

If this is not possible, shake as much moisture off the flysheet as possible then roll it up and pack it by itself, either in the tent bag or a bin liner, and pack it out with the main body of your rucksack, either under or strapped securely to the top of the rucksack lid.

Remove as much moisture and dirt from the groundsheet as possible, with a towel or cloth, before rolling up the rest of the tent and clean mud and dirt off pegs.

Back home, ensure the tent is cleaned and dried as soon as possible. Do not keep it rolled up in its bag for more than a few days as mould could form.

First, clean the tent. Use soap or a technical tent wash mixed with water and a sponge. Do not use a harsh detergent, which can strip the protective qualities from your tent and cause it to fade quicker.

Once clean, air dry on a washing line, or by re-pitching in a cool place such as a garage or in the garden. Sweep out any debris and dirt from the inner, such as food crumbs or stones.

Do not use a heat source such as a tumble dryer or radiator as this could melt the fabric or damage coatings.

Dry, clean and air all of your tent's component parts.

TENTS PEGS

Knock or wipe off the worst of the mud. If necessary wash them with a cloth in a bucket of soapy water and dry thoroughly. Replace broken or damaged pegs.

POLES

Check for damaged poles and repair or replace if necessary. Clean with a dry cloth. When folding poles, start from the centre to prevent excess strain on the shockcord. Replacement shockcord or poles can be obtained from outdoor stores.

GUYLINES

Check for fraying or loose knots and replace where necessary. It is worth having a couple of spare guylines packed with the tent.

ZIPS

Clean with a dry cloth and ensure they run freely. Zips are prone to seizing up in storage and specialist lubrication products can be applied to prevent this happening.

STORAGE

Once clean and dry, pack your tent away loosely in a cool, dry place, such as a cupboard, garage or attic.

A QUIET PITCH BELOW HILL OF CAT, ANGUS

SLEEPING BAGS & MATS

After the tent, the two most important bits of kit to take are a sleeping bag and sleeping mat. A lightweight bag will reduce weight carried and take up less space in the rucksack. Be sure it is going to be warm enough for the season/weather conditions and remember that, even in the height of the Scottish summer, the temperature at night can plummet. Sleeping bags are all seasonally rated and most offer information on the temperature range they are designed for.

It is vital to keep the sleeping bag dry at all times. Pack it in a waterproof liner (a bin bag will do) and do not rely solely on your rucksack to protect it from the elements. A wet sleeping bag can quickly turn a camping trip into an unpleasant ordeal. In colder weather it could lead to potentially life-threatening conditions like hypothermia.

If you decide to air your sleeping bag outside, avoid leaving it unattended just in case it blows away or falls on to damp ground, or rain starts to fall on to it.

A decent sleeping mat is essential. Not only will it iron out the lumps and bumps in the ground beneath you, but it will also offer insulation from the cold. Inexpensive foam mats are one lightweight option while self-inflating mats cost more but tend to take up less rucksack space.

CAMP COOKING

KIT LIST

With the tent, sleeping bag and mat taken care off, the rest of the wild camping kit list can be broken down into two categories – essentials and non-essentials.

The essentials, as the name suggests, are the important things that space should definitely be found for.

The non-essentials are not necessarily luxury items but are the bits and pieces that make wild camping more comfortable and enjoyable.

The essentials for a night or two should pack into a medium sized (40 litre) rucksack. For longer outings where food will take up more space a large (60 litre) rucksack will be necessary.

ESSENTIALS

- **Tent**
- **Sleeping bag**
- **Sleeping mat**
- **Warm jacket**
- **A complete change of clothing** – ensure this is kept dry
- **Waterproofs** – vital for all activities in the Scottish countryside
- **Torch** – a head torch is the most convenient form of illumination. Pack spare batteries and bulb too
- **Stove** – small and lightweight
- **Fuel** – pack enough for the trip
- **Lighter or matches** – pack at least two lighters as flints are notorious for breaking at the most inconvenient times. Ensure matches are stored in a waterproof container
- **Pan** – a plethora of tasty meals can be created in a single pan, which also doubles as a plate/bowl
- **Mug or cup**
- **Spoon** – there is very little that cannot be eaten with a spoon but go one better and buy a spork
- **Pocket knife**
- **Food and drink** – enough for the trip plus emergency rations
- **Toothbrush/washing kit**
- **Midge repellent**
- **Small trowel** – for toilet duties
- **Toilet paper** – biodegradable
- **Duct tape** – for on the spot repairs
- **Bin liners** – numerous uses. Handy for separate storage of dry and wet gear, for sitting on, for putting stuff on if the ground is wet and for carrying out rubbish

NON-ESSENTIALS

- **Luxury food and drink** – such as coffee, chocolate, etc
- **Plate/bowl**
- **Water carrying/storage bottle**

DOME TENT PITCHED BY LOCH SKEEN

- **Footwear** – a pair of shoes, sandals, etc, for wearing around the campsite
- **Extra clothing**
- **Pillow**
- **Towel**
- **Swimwear** – for those who plan to do some wild swimming (skinny dipping is a lightweight alternative)
- **Reading matter** – a book or magazine to while away the hours
- **MP3 player/tablet**
- **Firewood/coal/peat blocks** – for an open fire

PICK A PITCH

For beginners, the hardest thing about wild camping is finding a good pitch. If you are unfamiliar with the countryside – or even the country – it can be very difficult to ascertain exactly where to go.

Most wild campers are looking for a secluded and sheltered site a reasonable distance from the nearest road or community (although some will doubtless seek out wilder and more remote spots).

If it forms part of a walking, mountain biking or kayaking trip, it should be on or near the planned route. Good scenery and decent views are important while the ground itself should be flat and well drained. A source of running water close by is handy too.

There are many well-known and well-frequented wild campsites in Scotland. Some lie in popular walking and mountaineering areas while others line lochs or rivers.

CAMPING BY THE RIVER DEE NEAR LINN OF DEE

Studying maps offers some clues to possible pitches but you won't know what to expect until you get there. For some, this can add a sense of exploration and discovery to the whole process. For others, however, it might lead to bitter disappointment. A promising area of level ground lying in a sheltered valley might turn out to be an insect-infested bog or uneven grassland littered with rocks. A shady spot next to woodland could be a festering quagmire of sloppy mud and sheep shit.

Pitching on bad ground tends to have just one outcome – a sleepless night resulting in a thoroughly miserable time for all but the most optimistic who will view the experience, however awful, as character-building.

If you plan to seek out a potential site identified on a map, factor in extra time just in case it turns out to be unsuitable and you have to scour the area for an alternative.

To assist the novice, this book lists 25 potential pitches. Other useful sources of information include outdoor books and magazines, the internet, or friends, family or colleagues who spend time in the countryside and may be happy to pitch in with so some suggestions.

GRASSY RIVERSIDE PITCH IN GLEN MARK, ANGUS

HIGHER LEVEL CAMPING IN CANNESS GLEN, ANGUS

Another worthwhile option is to take a look at Scotland's network of mountain bothies. These remote refuges offer shelter to hillwalkers and mountaineers and they are situated all over Scotland. At the majority of locations it is possible to camp either next to the bothy or close by. If the weather is bad, you can retreat into the bothy to cook, sit or just chat with others who may be staying. A bothy is also a good back up if your tent gets damaged or you forget something vital, like the pegs.

Over time, you will discover your own perfect pitches. As with so many things in life, wild camping skills – including finding the best spots – develop with experience.

On arrival at your chosen site the first thing to do is survey the ground and find the best spot for the tent. A flat piece of dry ground with short grass offers ideal terrain. Avoid ground that slopes steeply and steer clear of boggy, marshy and reedy areas – they are all a haven for insects. If there is a slope, pitch so that when you are asleep your head is higher than your feet. If you pitch side on to a slope, you will spend the night sliding down into the tent wall.

Watercourses and lochsides are important sites for birds and animals so avoid the temptation to camp immediately beside them. Rivers and streams can also rise quickly in wet weather. Stay close enough to source water without need for a lengthy hike every time you fancy a brew but far enough away not to get flooded in the dead of night. Be aware too that water levels in hydro-electric reservoirs, of which there are many in Scotland, can rise and fall significantly.

If there is a 'no camping' sign, respect it and move on to another spot. If there are already other campers in the vicinity, pitch a reasonable distance away and remember that tents offer no sound insulation. Others have no desire to hear your nocturnal noises and doubtless you will be of the same mind.

Clear the ground of stones, twigs, pinecones, animal droppings and anything else that could lead to an uncomfortable night's sleep. Avoid heavy landscaping such as digging drainage ditches, clearing vegetation or uprooting large rocks or stones and always replace any rocks you do move in the same positions as you found them before you leave.

Also steer clear of ground where there are cowpats. As well as attracting flies and being smelly and unpleasant, they are a source of E-coli O157, a food poisoning bug that can kill or cause lasting damage to human health.

If there is any wind, check the direction it is coming from and pitch so it hits the rear of the tent first. Avoid setting the tent at right angles to the prevailing breeze as it will buffer the side and, if it gets stronger, could damage your tent.

Finally, get the tent up, unfurl your sleeping bag and make yourself at home.

DARK CLOUDS GATHER OVER SCOTS PINES

WEATHER

The Scottish weather is notoriously fickle. Wild camping is at the mercy of the elements, so check the forecast before you set off and be prepared for all eventualities, whatever the Met Office predicts.

On the whole Scotland is a fairly wet country (the west is generally wetter than the east) and summer days can offer everything from blisteringly hot sunshine to heavy downpours, sometimes in quick succession. Waterproofs are a must, whether worn or packed in the rucksack, while in winter additional warm clothing and a hat and gloves are essential.

If heavy rain and storm-force winds are forecast, there is no shame in postponing your trip – better that than enduring a sleepless night caught up in a maelstrom of snapping poles and ripping nylon.

Useful online weather forecasts include:

Mountain Weather Information Service - www.mwis.org.uk

Met Office - www.metoffice.gov.uk

BBC Weather - www.bbc.co.uk/weather

MIDGES

The biggest threat to the wild camping experience in Scotland is the midge. Active between May and September, these tiny biting insects can descend in clouds upon their unfortunate victims. While they present no danger to health, they are exceptionally irritating – particularly if you are trying to do something fiddly like pitch a tent – and bites quickly become very itchy.

Although midges have been around for thousands of years, climate change has extended their range and season. While once the Scottish Highlands and Islands were the most notorious hotspots, they are now found right across the country.

There are almost 40 species of biting midge in Scotland but only five feed on people. The Highland midge is the most vociferous.

They are fairly predictable little blighters. In general they prefer specific conditions and times of day – they are particularly partial to warm and damp conditions and, as such, are most active around dawn and dusk.

They tend to be found in damp and uncultivated places where there is a lot of undergrowth or thick vegetation, and areas where livestock is kept. Sheltered hollows and boggy ground and, after rain, forests and fields, are all happy hunting grounds for midges.

They are less keen on bright sunshine and wind – even the lightest of breezes will keep them at bay.

Some insect repellents are more effective than others. Smidge is one worth considering while a generous coating of Avon's Skin So Soft dry oil body spray works for many people. It is used by both the British Army and police in the Highlands.

Midges are drawn to humans and animals by the carbon dioxide we exhale and, while not breathing is a rather extreme way of avoiding them, you can lessen your attraction by wearing light coloured clothing, keeping bare skin covered and wearing a mesh midge hood.

Midges do not like smoke, whether from an open fire, pipe, cigar or cigarettes.

If all else fails the only remaining option is to retreat to your tent and zip yourself in.

Midge forecast - www.smidgeup.com/midge-forecast/

TICKS

Ticks are tiny parasites that are common in the countryside and wild campers are particularly at risk. They can attach themselves to animals, livestock, pets and humans and feed by biting through the skin and sucking blood.

They are most often found in long grass, rough vegetation, bracken and woodland and, although present throughout the year, are most active between May and September.

Once the tick has found a host and attached itself to the skin, it will suck up blood, enlarging the area of body behind its head. Left unchecked, the tick will eventually fall off. However, if you find a tick attached to yourself or your dog, it should be removed without delay.

The best way to remove a tick is with a tick twister, a little tool that clasps the insect in a V-shaped claw that is then twisted to bring it out. Some outdoor shops, pharmacies and vets sell them or they can be bought online (www.ticktwister.co.uk or www.otom.com)

To remove a tick with a pair of tweezers or fingernails, pull upwards slowly and constantly until the tick releases its grip. Avoid squeezing or crushing the tick as this may result in mouthparts being left in the skin, which could cause infection. Don't use a naked flame or chemicals to remove the tick. Once the tick is out, clean the area of the bite with an antiseptic cream.

To prevent ticks attaching themselves to you in the first place, avoid walking through long grass and rough vegetation and keep your skin covered by wearing long trousers and long-sleeved tops. If you have been walking through long grass or bracken, or have been camping wild, it is worth doing a thorough tick check at the end of the day, paying particular attention to areas like the legs and ankles, groin, armpits and scalp.

If you take a dog into the countryside regularly, there are various products available to protect it from ticks, so ask your vet. Be sure to check your pet over thoroughly at the end of the walk.

The vast majority of tick bites in humans simply lead to short-term skin irritation that can be treated with an antihistamine cream. However, a tiny minority of ticks carry bacteria that can cause Lyme's disease, a potentially debilitating condition.

Symptoms usually take a few days to several weeks to appear and can range from an expanding and often faint reddish rash around the bite area to flu-like symptoms, mild headaches, tiredness and joint and muscle pain. If you are at all concerned, contact your GP.

The chances of contracting Lyme's disease are very small. Even if an infected tick bites you, it will be several hours before it transmits the bacteria into your body, so timely removal is paramount. If you are infected, prompt treatment with antibiotics resolves the vast majority of cases. Again, a GP will be able to give you professional advice.

HORSEFLIES

Also known as clegs, horseflies are not particularly common in Scotland but if you do find yourself sharing ground with them they can be a real nuisance.

A relatively large flying insect, they tend to swarm in small numbers and, while not dangerous or a risk to health, they are particularly persistent and have a vicious bite which forms a large red and very itchy weal. If you are bitten, try to avoid scratching the itch and apply antihistamine cream.

Horseflies are most active on warm, sunny days between June and September.

VERMIN

To avoid attracting rats or mice to your campsite, dispose of waste food and water in a small pit cut out of the turf, well away from water sources and your tent. Cover the pit with the sod of turf after each use to keep flies off.

Store food carefully and keep fresh food and water in covered containers. Hang up food in a strong, sealed, poly bag where vermin cannot get to it.

Clean pots, pans and plates immediately after use, disposing of all food scraps in your pit. Empty food packaging should be washed out, crushed and stored in a sealed poly bag then carried home or to the nearest public bin for disposal.

WATER

Drinking water from hill and mountain streams in Scotland is generally safe, but there are some common-sense precautions to take. The cleanest water comes from small, fast flowing streams on high ground but you should always check a little way upstream first to make sure there is nothing untoward, like a dead sheep, in the waterway.

Avoid cloudy or muddy-looking streams or rivers and don't take water from streams crossing land where there is livestock, from areas of human activity, like farms or industrial sites, from forests or from still bodies of water like lochs or ponds. Check for tents upstream too as their occupants may inadvertently pollute the water.

If you are unsure, you can treat water to kill potentially dangerous bacteria and viruses. Boil for at least 10 minutes, or treat with water purification tablets. Alternatively, buy a water purifier, available in the form of a convenient bottle.

CAMPFIRES

Campfires are a great part of wild camping but can potentially damage the environment. A good fire should be kept small, under control and be supervised at all times.

Before setting a fire, lift out turfs from the ground and set aside. Surround the fire site with rocks to ensure it remains contained. Carry in kindling and logs and never cut down or damage live wood. Avoid using fallen timber too as it forms an important part of the ecosystem, providing a home to insects and smaller animals.

Ensure the fire is well away from tents as flying sparks could easily hole or ignite flammable nylon.

Don't over stock the fire and ensure it is completely out before turning in for the night. Once a fire is finished, recover the burned ground with the cut turfs. Remove all traces of an open fire before you head off.

Out-of-control fires are one of the most destructive consequences of camping and you may find yourself being held liable for any damage caused. Never light an open fire in woodland or forestry or on peaty ground, grassland and moor. Also avoid setting a fire near to buildings or bothies where damage can easily be caused by something as small as a stray spark.

Ideally a campfire should be avoided and a stove used for cooking.

THROW ANOTHER BRANCH ON THE FIRE

GOING IN THE GREAT OUTDOORS

Going to the toilet, whether for a simple pee or a more time-consuming bowl evacuation, is something all wild campers will have to do at some point or another on their travels. While you may find public toilets in car parks and at visitor centres, save for the occasional bothy composting toilet, there are none in the hills.

First off, never miss an opportunity to use a proper toilet, even if you don't actually need to go. If there is one at the start of the walk, or at any point along the way, try to squeeze out a deposit.

Once in the wilds, if you need to pee, find cover in trees or bushes well away from paths, buildings, rivers, streams and lochs. Urine is less harmful than excrement but it does smells unpleasant if too many people choose the same spot.

If you need to defecate, do so at least 50 metres from paths, 200 metres from buildings such as huts and bothies and at least 30m from streams.

Using a small trowel, dig a hole at least 20cms deep. Do your business and wipe down with biodegradable toilet paper. Pop that in the hole atop the crap and then carefully (to avoid any splattering) fill the hole back in.

If you can't dig a hole (the ground may be too hard or frozen), spread your waste out thinly and cover with soil or leaf mould to help it decompose faster. This may not be a pleasant task, but it is a necessary one!

Try to confine your motions to low ground as vegetation on higher ground is more sensitive and takes longer to recover if disturbed.

If there is snow on the ground, clear this first and then dig your hole. Burying excrement under snow is bad practice, as it will only reappear when the snow melts.

Tampons and sanitary towels take a long time to decompose, even when buried (animals may dig them up too), and should be bagged up and carried out to the nearest bin. Place a teabag in to help absorb odours.

In the interests of good hygiene, take antiseptic hand washing gel or cleansing wipes to clean your hands.

For campers who want to leave absolutely no trace of their passing, consider bagging up your own poo and carrying it out. In the Cairngorms National Park, an ongoing initiative that encourages people to remove their waste in light, rigid biodegradable plastic screw top pots has been proving successful.

The Cairngorm Snow White project was launched in 2007 in a bid to combat the increasing amounts of human excrement found on the mountains after the spring thaw. Wild campers and people staying out in snow holes leave much of it behind.

The waste is not only unsightly and smelly but also increases the risk of illness stemming from people coming into contact with contaminated snow. There are also concerns over the impact on the local biodiversity and possible contamination of watercourses.

On arrival, visitors collect a free pot from the ranger base at the Cairngorm Ski Area. On departure, these are deposited in a purpose built 'poo chute' that leads to a treatment plant.

The pots have been specially sourced for this project and are made from corn starch. These break up in the treatment facility. The pots are watertight and airtight and come with a carry pouch. They are available from the ranger base at the Coire Cas car park (grid ref NH 990060).

Unfortunately, pots of this type are not widely available but may become more common in the future as folk become increasingly aware of the impact human waste can have on the countryside.

STAY DRY

When it rains, keeping the inside of your tent dry is both a priority and a challenge. A good tent is unlikely to leak but when you climb in you should take care not to take water in with you.

Take waterproofs and boots off before you go into the inner tent and leave them in the porch area. Do likewise with your rucksack if it is wet. If your clothes are soaked through, then take them off and towel yourself down before crawling into your sleeping bag.

If there is no room for your rucksack or boots in the porch of your tent, pack them in a large polythene sack (an orange survival bag is great for this), close it up and leave it outside.

CLEAN CAMPING

At the end of your stay in the great outdoors, don't leave anything behind. Make sure you leave the wilderness as you found it. Pack up all rubbish and unused food and take it home with you (or to the nearest public litter bin) and scour your pitch for debris such as spent matches or stray tent pegs before you depart. Don't bury or attempt to conceal rubbish under stones as this can harm wildlife.

Enjoy the land, but leave it as you found it. Leave no trace, other than footprints.

LEGAL STUFF

Although it has long been recognised by the majority of people as a legitimate activity, with campers north of the border enjoying far more freedom to pitch up in the great outdoors than in other parts of the UK, wild camping was finally recognised by the Land Reform (Scotland) Act of 2003. For the first time, this piece of legislation established a legal right to camp in the countryside out with the bounds of formal campsites.

The Act covers a wide range of outdoor pursuits, including walking, mountain biking and backpacking. In fact, anyone venturing into the Scottish countryside will benefit from its enlightened approach. The access rights depend on responsible behaviour, designed to protect the environment, wildlife and those who live and work in the countryside. To help people enjoy Scotland's outdoors responsibly, the Scottish Outdoor Access Code was drawn up as part of the bill.

Scottish Outdoor Access Code

1. Take responsibility for your own actions
2. Respect people's privacy and peace of mind
3. Help land managers and others to work safely and effectively
4. Care for your environment
5. Keep your dog under proper control
6. Take extra care if you are organising an event or running a business and ask the landowner's advice.

It basically all boils down to common sense. Pitch away from houses and farms and don't camp in fields where crops are growing or in fields where there is livestock. Be as unobtrusive as possible and leave no trace of your campsite when you move on.

This freedom to roam and pitch does have some restrictions. Apart from ground that is obviously farmed, Scotland has a good many sporting estates where animals like red deer and birds like grouse are shot, whether for sport or conservation. Deer management takes place at various times of the year but the most sensitive period is the stag stalking season which runs from July 1 to October 20. The grouse shooting season runs from August 12 to December 10. Most of this activity takes place on open hillside and tends to be away from popular walking routes.

Other exceptions include land used by the military, school grounds and land close to buildings (other than mountain bothies or huts).

Despite the presence of this legislation, it is still not uncommon to see 'no camping' signs in the Scottish countryside. Responsible behaviour suggests that such spots should be avoided, although in some cases it is difficult to justify the continuing existence of such signs.

SPECIFIC BYELAWS

One major exception to the code is areas where byelaws have been introduced that specifically prohibit wild camping. The most notable example of this in Scotland (at the time of writing) is in the Loch Lomond and the Trossachs National Park.

Following problems caused by large groups of campers congregating on beaches and in woodland along the shorelines of various lochs, byelaws were brought into force on June 1, 2011, after a lengthy period of consultation.

They make it an offence to pitch up overnight out with designated campsites in designated Camping Management Zones, which cover about four per cent of the land within the park. In the zones, camping is allowed in designated areas, but only with a permit.

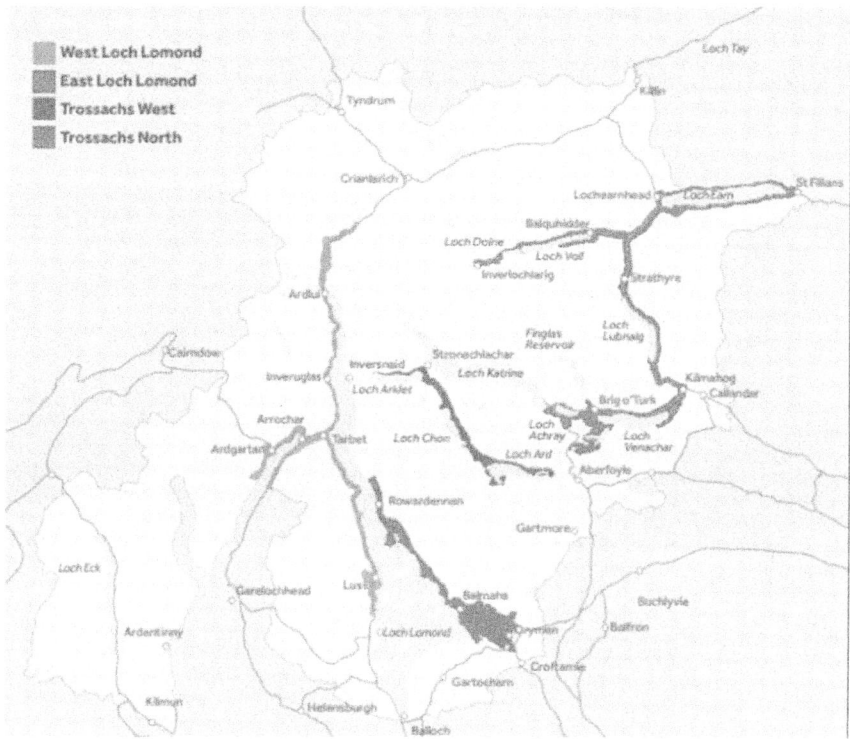

CAMPING MANAGEMENT ZONES

The restrictions are seasonal and run annually from March 1 to the end of September. They apply to all forms of overnight shelter including tents, wigwams, bivouacs, gazebos and tarpaulin shelters and also prohibit people from sleeping overnight in a motor vehicle. Breaches can result in a fine of £500.

CAMPING MANAGEMENT ZONES

Camping Management Zones are currently in place at the following locations within the park:

- Along the south-eastern shoreline of Loch Lomond, stretching north from Drymen to Ptarmigan Lodge, and along most of the western shoreline of the loch, extending north into Glen Falloch.

LOCH LUBNAIG

- Around the head of Loch Long, extending through the glen lying between Arrochar and Tarbet.

- Along the northern shoreline of Loch Arklet, extending south through Loch Ard Forest to cover Loch Chon and Loch Ard.

- Along the northern shoreline and part of the southern shoreline of Loch Venachar, extending west through Achray Forest to the eastern end of Loch Katrine, covering Loch Drunkie and Loch Achray.

- Along most of the eastern shoreline and parts of the western shoreline of Loch Lubnaig, extending north through Strathyre to Lochearnhead.

- Along most of the northern shoreline and parts of the southern shoreline of Loch Voil, extending west to Inverlochlarig and east to Kingshouse.

- The entire northern and southern shorelines of Loch Earn.

Within these Camping Management Zones there are defined areas where tents can be pitched but only if a permit has been first been obtained. These cost £3 per tent per night with a maximum stay of three nights at any one location. They can be booked up to eight weeks in advance (www.lochlomond-trossachs.org/things-to-do/camping/get-a-permit/). Campers can pitch up from 1pm but must leave by 11am on the day of departure.

LOCH ARD

Within the park there are basic campsites at The Cabin, on the shores of Loch Lubnaig, and at Loch Chon and Loch Achray. On Loch Lomond there is a small campsite on the island of Inchcailloch and a larger one run by the Forestry Commission at Sallochy Bay.

While you can be fined up to £500 for pitching in a Camping Management Zone without a permit, if caught it is more likely that you will simply be asked by either a park ranger or police officer to take your tent down and move on.

LEGISLATION

With responsible behaviour at its core, the Land Reform (Scotland) Act of 2003 and its access rights are not an excuse to justify behaviour that may be an offence under other legislation and irresponsible campers may find their actions contravene other laws.

The following is a list of Scottish legislation and offences relating to the great outdoors.

TRESPASS

Collective trespass remains on the statute book under the **Criminal Justice and Public Order Act 1994**. It states that if two or more people are trespassing with the intention of staying on land for any time and have caused damage, or used threatening, abusive or insulting words or behaviour, or have between them six or more vehicles, they can be told to leave by the police. If they fail to do so, they are breaking the law.

Mass trespass is covered by the same act. It makes it an offence to organise or participate in any 'trespassory assembly' which has been prohibited by a council in consultation with the police. Such a ban may only be ordered for a period of up to four days, where 20 or more people would be gathering without the landowners permission, and which may result in serious disruption to the life of the community, or serious damage to land or a building of historical, archaeological or scientific importance.

Landowners – or indeed anyone else – who does anything to intimidate and deter people or tries to prevent or disrupt their activity if they are not breaking the law can be prosecuted under the same act.

The **Civic Government (Scotland) Act 1982** makes it an offence for any person on foot in a public place to wilfully obstruct the lawful passage of any other person. A public place is defined as any place to which members of the public have unrestricted access.

WILDLIFE AND PLANTS

Under the **Wildlife & Countryside Act 1981** and **The Conservation (Natural Habitats etc) Regulations 1994**, it is an offence to pick, uproot or destroy any plant in Schedule 8 or to uproot any plant not in that Schedule.

The **Wildlife & Countryside Act 1981** and **The Conservation Regulations 1994** also cover offences relating to the killing or injuring or any wild bird, the capture or keeping of any wild bird, destroying or taking eggs, or destroying, damaging or taking the nest of any wild bird whilst it is in use or being built.

Legislation designed to prevent damage or disturbance to protected species of animals is also contained within the **Wildlife & Countryside Act 1981** and **The Conservation Regulations 1994**. For protected species, it is an offence to kill or injure the animal, capture or keep the animal, destroy, damage or obstruct access to its place of shelter, and disturb the animal while it is using its place of shelter. Other offences relate to badgers, bats, deer, seals, whales and dolphins. For protected species such as bats, otters, wildcats, great crested newts and natterjack toads, under European legislation it is an offence to capture, kill or disturb the animal, take or destroy its eggs or damage or destroy its breeding site or resting place.

DOGS

The behaviour of dogs is covered by a number of pieces of legislation. Under the **Civic Government (Scotland) Act 1982**, if you are in charge of a dog and allow it to foul a footpath or footway, or a grass verge maintained by a council and next to a footpath/footway, or any place maintained by a local authority for recreational or sporting purposes you are breaking the law.

Perhaps more pertinent to dog owners in the great outdoors, you commit an offence under the **Dog Fouling (Scotland) Act 2003** if you do not immediately remove your dog's faeces in any public open place.

If your dog worries livestock on any agricultural land you are guilty of an offence under the **Dogs (Protection of Livestock) Act 1953**. Worrying includes a dog attacking or chasing livestock, or being loose in a field where there are sheep.

If a farmer or landowner spots your dog worrying his livestock and subsequently kills or injures the animal, he will find a defence for his actions under the **Animals (Scotland) Act 1987**.

VANDALISM

This is covered by the **Criminal Justice (Scotland) Act 1980**. Anyone who, without reasonable excuse, wilfully or recklessly destroys or damages someone else's property commits this offence. Anyone who demolishes, destroys or damages a Scheduled Monument (unless they have permission from Scottish Ministers) can be taken to court under the **Ancient Monuments & Archaeological Areas Act 1979**.

FIRES

If you plan to light a campfire in the great outdoors, there are a few pieces of legislation that should be heeded. The **Trespass (Scotland) Act 1865** makes it an offence to light a fire on or near any private road, on enclosed or cultivated land or in or near any woodland or forestry plantation without the consent of the owner or land manager.

Under the **Civic Government (Scotland) Act 1982** it is an offence to lay or light a fire in a public place if it is likely to endanger any other person, give reasonable cause for alarm or annoyance, or present a risk to property.

LITTER

Dropping litter is covered by the **Environmental Protection Act 1990**, which makes it an offence to leave litter in any public open place.

OFF-ROAD DRIVING

The **Environmental Protection Act 1990** also extends to driving a vehicle off road. It is against the law to drive a motor vehicle (without lawful authority) on land of any description that does not form part of a road), or on a footpath or bridleway (except in an emergency). It is OK, however, to drive a motor vehicle on to land within 15 yards of a road to park.

EARLY SPRING PITCH WITH A VIEW OF MONEGA HILL, ANGUS

FISHING

For those planning to catch their supper, be aware of fishing rights and the legislation covering this activity. Under the **Salmon & Freshwater Fisheries (Protection) (Scotland) Act 1951** and **Freshwater & Salmon Fisheries (Scotland) Act 1976**, fishing for salmon or sea trout without a permit is a criminal offence. Fishing for brown trout and other freshwater fish without a permit is only an offence in an area covered by a Protection Order. Check before you cast off.

The **Salmon Fisheries (Scotland) Act 1868** makes it an offence to wilfully disturb any salmon spawn, or spawning beds and shallows where salmon spawn may be.

Around water, respect the **Water (Scotland) Act 1980**. If you deliberately or accidentally pollute any spring, well or adit used, or likely to be used, for human consumption, domestic purposes or the manufacture of food or drink for human consumption you are guilty of an offence.

The **Control of Pollution Act 1974** deals with anyone who causes or allows any poisonous, noxious or polluting matter, or any solid waste matter to enter surface or ground water.

HUNTING

Under the **Game (Scotland) Act 1832** it is an offence to trespass on land without the owner's permission in search of game, woodcock, snipe, wild ducks or rabbits during the daytime while the **Night Poaching Act 1828** makes it illegal to hunt game on any land, whether open or enclosed, or on any public road. It is also an offence to go on any land at night with a gun for the purpose of catching or killing game.

SAFETY

Finally, under the **Health & Safety at Work Act 1974**, it an offence to interfere intentionally with or misuse anything provided for the safety, health or welfare of people.

In addition to these specific acts, other crimes such as breach of the peace or malicious mischief are covered by common law while cyclists and horseriders are expected to follow the Highway Code when on public roads.

THE SITES

SANDWOOD BAY, SUTHERLAND	44	WHITE BRIDGE, GLEN DEE	73
KEARVAIG, SUTHERLAND	46	FALLS OF TARF, GLEN TILT	75
VALLAY, NORTH UIST	48	DERRY LODGE, GLEN DERRY	77
CAMSUNARY, ISLE OF SKYE	50	ALTANOUR LODGE, GLEN EY	79
CORUISK, ISLE OF SKYE	52	LOCH CHON, TRINAFOUR	82
CORAL BEACH, ISLE OF SKYE	54	LOCH NAN EUN, GLEN SHEE	84
ISLE OF RUM	56	LOCHAN OISINNEACH MOR, DUNKELD	86
STEALL MEADOWS, GLEN NEVIS	59	GLEN DOLL	88
CREAGUAINEACH LODGE, LOCH TREIG	62	GLEN MARK	90
STAOINEAG, NEAR LOCH TREIG	64	AUCHINTAPLE LOCH, GLEN ISLA	92
CORROUR OLD LODGE, RANNOCH MOOR	66	CARLINGHEUGH BAY, ARBROATH	94
LUBNACLACH, RANNOCH MOOR	68	SIDLAW HILLS, DUNDEE	96
RUIGH-AITEACHAIN, GLEN FESHIE	70		

SANDWOOD BAY, SUTHERLAND

Sandwood Bay is one of the most beautiful and wildest spots in the British Isles. Accessible only on foot or by bike, it boasts some of the finest coastal scenery in Scotland. Between Sandwood and Shiegra the cliffs rise to over 90 metres in height and, at the southern end of the bay, there is a 60-metre high sea stack, Am Buachaille. Inland, behind a complex system of dunes, Sandwood Loch cuts a rippling swathe through the landscape.

Overlooking the loch, Sandwood Lodge housed well-to-do Victorian and Edwardian travellers, drawn to the area by the lure of hunting, shooting and fishing. Later shepherds occupied the outpost before it was abandoned. Despite the onset of dereliction, the crumbling cottage served as a bothy well into the 1980s. The ruins have since been stabilised and there are no plans to rebuild it.

Sandwood also has strong links with the supernatural. There are many mysterious and ghostly tales associated with the area. Some owe their existence to the remarkable isolation while others are rooted in actual events. Sightings of mermaids were numerous right up to the start of the 20th century. Historically, mermaids were said to lure seafarers on to the rocks and scores of ships have run aground or been wrecked at Sandwood over the centuries.

In the 1920s, author Seton Gordon visited the bay as part of research that led, in 1935, to the publication of his classic travel book *Highways & Byways in the West Highlands*.

He wrote: 'I was astonished at the number of wrecks which lie on the fine sand of this bay. Some of the vessels lie almost buried in the sand far above the reach of the highest tide'.

The proliferation of wrecks and the many lives lost have fuelled various supernatural tales. One of the bay's most famous and enduring ghosts is linked to a shipwreck, a Polish vessel. Sporting a dark beard and clad in sea boots, a sailor's cap and a brass buttoned tunic the spectre has been witnessed wandering the beach by crofters, fishermen and walkers.

The walk to the bay begins at a public car park (with toilets) at Blairmore, on the minor road linking Kinlochbervie and Sheigra. A track and then path leads north, passing a string of small lochs, to Sandwood Lodge. The route then descends through pasture and dunes to the beach. Pitch up amid the dunes or select a higher spot by the lodge before savouring the sun set over the vast Atlantic Ocean.

SITE STATS

GRID REF	NC 220653	OS LANDRANGER	9
		OS EXPLORER	446
WALK IN	6.25km		
HOW TO GET THERE		Walk or cycle in from Blairmore, north of Kinlochbervie	
NEAREST REFRESHMENTS		Kinlochbervie Hotel (10km)	
NEAREST ACCOMMODATION		Kinlochbervie Hotel (10km)	
NEARBY BOTHIES		Strathchailleach Bothy (NC 249658) and Strathan Bothy (NC 247612)	

KEARVAIG, SUTHERLAND

Cape Wrath is the most north-westerly point on the Scottish mainland. A lonely lighthouse – the only occupied building for miles around – clings precariously to the weather-beaten rocks. To the east, Clo Mor, the highest sea cliffs on the mainland, mount their defence against the swirling froth of the Atlantic. Close by, nestling in the shadow of these towering bluffs is Kearvaig, a tiny bay bathed in solitude.

Accessed by a rough track leading down from the lighthouse road, is Kearvaig House, an open bothy that overlooks a slender arc of golden sand. Flanking the old cottage, there are numerous good spots for a tent, all enjoying sea views and access to a splendid beach. Offshore is Kearvaig Stack, also known as The Cathedral due to its two rock spires and natural window.

To reach the bay, visitors must first negotiate Kyle of Durness. Between May and September, a small ferry makes the 10-minute crossing. From the Kyle, Kearvaig is a 12km walk or cycle away, on the minor road leading to the lighthouse. During the summer, there is a minibus service to Cape Wrath. Both this and the ferry are weather dependent.

The route crosses a Ministry of Defence firing range and access may be restricted when exercises are underway. For information on ferry and bus times and military activity, visit www.visitcapewrath.com.

SITE STATS

GRID REF	NC 292727	OS LANDRANGER	9
		OS EXPLORER	446
WALK IN	12km		
HOW TO GET THERE		Walk, cycle or hop aboard the Cape Wrath minibus	
NEAREST REFRESHMENTS		Ozone Café, Cape Wrath Lighthouse (7.5km)	
NEAREST ACCOMMODATION		Hotels, B&Bs, hostel and campsite in Durness (5km from Kyle of Durness)	
NEARBY BOTHIES		Kearvaig (NC 292727)	

VALLAY, NORTH UIST

Located off the coast of North Uist, in the Outer Hebridges, Vallay is a small, low-lying tidal island that can be reached on foot, but only at low tide. When the sea rolls in across the wide strip of sand separating it from its neighbour, it is completely cut off, making it the ideal location for a secluded camp.

Vallay was once home to 60 people who farmed its fertile fields and grazed cattle and sheep on the grassy meadows. The ruins of their crofts and cottages still stand, alongside the prominent but derelict structure of Vallay House.

Built in 1902 on a windswept terrace overlooking the bay of Traigh Bhalaigh, the crowstepped Edwardian mansion was home to the island's then owner – author, archaeologist and naturalist Erskine Beveridge who made his fortune as a textile manufacturer, based in Dunfermline, Fife. He equipped the property with all the fashionable mod cons of its day, including central heating, and had water piped over from a reservoir on North Uist.

Beveridge spent his summers on Vallay and, when he died in 1920, the island passed to his son. However, he drowned crossing the causeway in

1944 and the property was abandoned. Today, it stands vacant and derelict, although the island itself is still farmed and grazed by cattle.

The two kilometre hike to Vallay begins at Aird Glas on the A865, west of Malacleit, where a track dips to the shoreline and heads north across the sand to the islet of Torogaigh. Curving a little to the left, it continues in a straight line past the islet of Stangram and on towards ruins lying to the right of Vallay House, itself a prominent landmark.

Once on Vallay, coastal pitches on the north side of the island, where there are some beautiful bays of white sand, abound while more exposed perches affording glorious sea views can be found on the various headlands.

SITE STATS

GRID REF	NF 774759	OS LANDRANGER 18
		OS EXPLORER 454
WALK IN	2km	
HOW TO GET THERE		At low tide, walk 2km across the sand from Aird Glas
NEAREST REFRESHMENTS		Lochmaddy (22km)
NEAREST ACCOMMODATION		Hotel and B&Bs in Lochmaddy (22km)
NEARBY BOTHIES		None

CAMSUNARY, ISLE OF SKYE

Arguably one of the finest bays on Skye, Camasunary offers the wild camper a wealth of possibilities. Above the stony shoreline a vast expanse of flat grass extends inland towards the rocky southern flank of Bla Bheinn.

If the weather is good, a seafront pitch with views over Loch Scavaig to the islands of Soay and, further away, Rum, is the order of the day. It conditions are less favourable a more sheltered inland spot might be preferable as this is an exposed spot.

Access to the bay is relatively straightforward. The shortest and most direct route is from Kilmarie, on the minor road linking Broadford and Elgol.

A 4km long track, built by the army in 1968 to allow better emergency access to the southeast side of the Black Cuillin range, crosses crofting land and rocky hillside. Although rough underfoot, the terrain is generally firm and it presents no navigational challenges.

A second option is to follow the signed coastal path north from Elgol. It is a pleasant 5km tramp with excellent views over Loch Scavaig to the Cuillin.

The former MBA bothy at the western end of the bay has been replaced by a new bothy, 1km away at the eastern end of the bay.

SITE STATS

GRID REF	NG 512188	OS LANDRANGER	32
		OS EXPLORER	411
WALK IN	4km		
HOW TO GET THERE		Walk in from car park at Kilmarie, on B8083 Broadford to Elgol road, or follow Loch Scavaig coastal path north from Elgol	
NEAREST REFRESHMENTS		Broadford (26km)	
NEAREST ACCOMMODATION		B&Bs in Elgol (5km)	
NEARBY BOTHIES		Camsunary (NG 517183)	

CORUISK, ISLE OF SKYE

Enveloped by the brooding shadow of the Black Cuillin, this pitch occupies a small chunk of land separating Loch Coruisk from Loch Scavaig on the southern coast of Skye. The ground is flat and grassy and nestles amid some of the country's most dramatic upland scenery.

The site, which sits next to whitewashed Coruisk Memorial Hut (a locked climbing hut) is well placed for ascents of Sgurr na Stri, Druim nan Ramh, The Dubhs, Gars-bheinn and a traverse of the Cuillin Ridge. Rock climbing of all grades can be found close by while a low-level walk around the shoreline of Loch Coruisk is highly recommended.

The calm waters of adjacent Loch na Cuilce are frequently used as a safe anchorage by yachts and there is plenty of marine wildlife in the area, including otters and seals.

There are a number of ways to reach this site. The easiest is to hop aboard one of the tourist boats that ply Loch Scavaig from Elgol. These land at a pier on Loch na Cuilce, adjacent to the site.

From Sligachan, on the road between Broadford and Portree, a 12km trek follows tracks and paths through Glen Sligachan.

A more challenging hike is possible from the east but this requires a short scramble over the Bad Step and a potentially difficult river crossing. Set off from Kilmarie, on the B8083 Broadford to Elgol road, and follow the track west to the bay at Camasunary.

At the western end of the bay, where the Abhainn Camus Fhionnairigh enters tidal Loch Scavaig, there used to be a rickety suspension bridge. It is now gone, washed out during a storm. If the water level is low, the crossing is straightforward. If it is high, it is much more difficult. Once over, a narrow path – boggy in places – follows the coastline around Rubha Ban to the Bad Step, a slanting crack spanning a huge slab of rock. It is a short but exposed traverse above open water.

SITE STATS

GRID REF	NG 487197	OS LANDRANGER	32
		OS EXPLORER	411
WALK IN	12km		
HOW TO GET THERE		Walk in from Sligachan via Glen Sligachan and Loch Coruisk	
NEAREST REFRESHMENTS		Sligachan Hotel (12km)	
NEAREST ACCOMMODATION		Sligachan Hotel (12km)	
NEARBY BOTHIES		Camsunary (NG 517183)	

CORAL BEACH, ISLE OF SKYE

Visually stunning, Coral Beach is not, as its name suggests, formed from coral. Rather the swathe of bright white coastline and tropical blue water results from the crushed bleached skeletons of Red Coralline seaweed, which grows out on the reef by the tiny offshore Island of Lampay.

The coralline grows exceptionally slowly but, thanks to the power of the sea and the passage of time, it has created this unique and really rather magical bay.

The walk in, from a small car park by the crofts of Claigan, is short, a good track crossing coastal grazing land to the beach and a small hill – Cnoc Mor a'Ghrobain – which crowns the headland.

The beach is at its best on a sunny day when the tide is out and, at very low tide, it is possible to cross a coral causeway to uninhabited Lampay.

Once clear of the grazing land that flanks the approach, there are plenty of potential pitches on the grassland above the beach and around Cnoc Mor a'Ghrobain, which offers some shelter from the prevailing wind.

SITE STATS

GRID REF	NG 223551	**OS LANDRANGER**	23
		OS EXPLORER	407
WALK IN	2km		
HOW TO GET THERE		From Dunvegan follow A850 then minor road 7km north to car park at Claigan. Go through gate and walk 2km north on track to beach	
NEAREST REFRESHMENTS		Dunvegan (7km)	
NEAREST ACCOMMODATION		Hotels and B&Bs in Dunvegan (7km)	
NEARBY BOTHIES		None	

ISLE OF RUM

Rum is a mysterious place, a curiosity abandoned to the wrath of the Atlantic Ocean by a landowner who once took such pleasure from the seclusion his island and money afforded. For much of the 20th century, only the privileged guests of the Bullough family were allowed to step ashore and marvel at the wonders of this Hebridean enclave.

In the 1950s, however, the family found they could no longer maintain the sporting estate and it was sold to the nation. Now visitors are welcome to step ashore. But the air of isolation remains. If you are looking for solitude, free of modern day intrusions, Rum is the place to go.

It is a perfect destination for hillwalking and scrambling. The Rum Cuillin, a collection of jagged volcanic peaks, ranks as one of the best ridge traverses in Britain, challenging slopes of boulder and scree leading to spectacular summits offering unrivalled panoramas.

The island is the largest of the Small Isles and is managed as a nature reserve by Scottish Natural Heritage. Open daily, Rum Visitor Centre, located on the lower shore road near the old pier, is the best place to start exploring.

Wild camping is permitted anywhere on Rum and at any time of year. Fires, however, are not allowed. A chat with the island's community ranger (the ranger post is at the village hall) is always helpful before setting out.

The island has a formal camping ground, a rough and ready site close to the old ferry pier. Pitches are arranged along the shoreline of Loch Scresort and there are toilets, showers and washing basins. It is wild camping with a few mod cons, which also include two pods and a BBQ cabin.

Wilder places to pitch on the island are by the bothy at Dibidil, by the ruins of Papadil Lodge, by the bay at Harris and at Guirdil Bay, where there is also a bothy.

Pack plenty of midge repellent as the island is blighted by the insects.

SITE STATS

GRID REF	NM 406991	OS LANDRANGER	39
		OS EXPLORER	397

WALK IN

HOW TO GET THERE — Caledonian MacBrayne *MV Loch Nevis* sails from Mallaig to Rum five times a week in summer and four times a week in winter

NEAREST REFRESHMENTS — Tea Shop in Village Hall

NEAREST ACCOMMODATION — Rum Bunkhouse
Ivy Cottage Guesthouse

NEARBY BOTHIES — Dibidil (NM 393928)
Guirdil (NG 320014)

STEALL MEADOWS, GLEN NEVIS

Steall sits at the top of one of the most impressive little gorges in Scotland. A short walk from a car park at the end of the Glen Nevis road, the path squeezes up through a steep-sided tree-lined chasm of rock.

The river, strewn with giant boulders, falls away to the right as the path continues on its precipitous course. This is an easy but wonderfully adventurous ramble. In places steps, handrails and boardwalks assist. Take care with your footing, particularly if you are carrying a heavy pack, and be prepared to join the lengthy procession of tourists who troop through the gorge during the summer season.

The way emerges from the ravine into a green oasis of calm. It is a spectacular place, a hanging valley hemmed in by high mountains, glistening streams and waterfalls cascading over silver rock. It is a view to savour and one that very nearly disappeared in the 1960s.

A decade earlier The North of Scotland Hydro-Electric Board was scouting out locations for new power stations. The authority set its sights on Glen Nevis and drew up plans that, had they gone ahead, would have radically transformed the landscape.

The board wanted to build a 240-foot high dam across Steall Gorge, creating a mile and a half long reservoir. The existing path through upper Glen Nevis was to be realigned along the northern shore of the reservoir and the Glen Nevis road was to be extended from the existing road end car park up to a viewpoint adjacent to the dam.

In 1960 the board submitted its scheme to the Secretary of State for Scotland for submission to parliament. However, objections were quickly raise, the vast majority relating to the impact the project would have on the landscape and amenity value of the glen.

In the end, public opposition and waning government enthusiasm for hydroelectric power saw the proposals shelved. The Steall flats, the gorge and the famous Steall Falls – which would have been halved in size – were saved.

There is plenty to see here. Steall Falls (or An Steall Bàn, which translates from Gaelic as 'the White Spout') is accessed by crossing a wire bridge below Lochaber Mountaineering Club's Steall Hut (a locked climbing hut). With a single drop of 120 metres, it is Britain's second highest waterfall.

A short hike up the glen reveals the ruins of Steall Lodge. Once the highest building in the glen, it sits above the convergence of the Allt Coire Guibhsachan and the Water of Nevis. Old photographs reveal a long, single-storey cottage structure with adjacent outbuildings once sat here.

Nearby, a wooden footbridge offers safe passage over the Allt Coire Guibhsachan. Constructed in 1982 by the R.E. Troop of Oxford University Officers Training Corps, the bridge was renovated in July 2011 by the John Muir Trust, a conservation charity, which owns the land.

Prior to 1982, there was a rudimentary crossing consisting of tree trunks slung across the stream but in the 1970s a handrail was added. This is an important bridge for while the Allt Coire Guibhsachan may appear benign for much of the year, melting snow from the corries above transforms it into a turbulent cascade when in spate.

SITE STATS

GRID REF	NN 180685	OS LANDRANGER	41
		OS EXPLORER	392

WALK IN   1.5km

HOW TO GET THERE   From the public car park at the end of the Glen Nevis road, a path leads up through Steall Gorge

NEAREST REFRESHMENTS   Fort William (12km)

NEAREST ACCOMMODATION   Glen Nevis Youth Hostel (8km)

NEARBY BOTHIES   Meanach (NN 266685)

CREAGUAINEACH LODGE, LOCH TREIG

Overlooking Loch Trieg, Creaguaineach Lodge is uninhabited and securely boarded. However, the land around this lonely two-storey cottage, sheltered by a stand of mature larch trees, is ideal for camping. Two accessible outbuildings offer additional shelter, although neither are particularly weather tight.

The walk in from Corrour Station is straightforward, although the initial section of the route can be wet and muddy. The track descends to Loch Treig where a rougher road skirts the southern shore. The way rises gently, curving round the northern flank of Garbh Chnapan before descending gently towards Creaguaineach Lodge.

Ahead of the lodge, a rickety wooden bridge spans the Abhainn Rath. Cross this and bear right through a copse of pines to reach the lodge. Once an important drove stance and more recently a shooting lodge, the building now lies empty.

Despite appearing to be a natural feature of the landscape, Loch Treig was created in the 1920s as part of a major hydroelectric scheme constructed by the British Aluminium Company to power their smelter in Fort William. From the dam at the northern end of the loch, water travels through a 24km long pipeline – where additional water is collected along the way – before descending the steep western shoulder of Ben Nevis to the turbine house.

Employing over 170 people and run by the Australian-based company Rio Tinto, the plant currently produces around 40,000 tonnes of aluminium each year.

If the water level is low, the remains of old farming enclosures and walled fields reveal themselves below the lodge.

SITE STATS

GRID REF	NN 309689	OS LANDRANGER	41
		OS EXPLORER	385
WALK IN	6km		
HOW TO GET THERE		Walk in from Corrour Station, following track signed for Fort William	
NEAREST REFRESHMENTS		Licensed café/restaurant at Corrour Station House (6km)	
NEAREST ACCOMMODATION		Corrour Station House (6km) or Loch Ossian SYHA (8km)	
NEARBY BOTHIES		Staoineag (NN 296678)	

STAOINEAG, NEAR LOCH TREIG

While much of the immediate ground around Staoineag bothy is boggy, infested with reeds and generally rather uninviting, the grassy flats by the side of the Abhainn Rath below the cottage are ideal for camping. In this isolated and out of the way spot you are unlikely to encounter many others and, in bad weather, the bothy (accessible by stepping stones across the river) offers a good place to cook and eat before spending the night under canvas.

From Corrour to Creaguaineach Lodge the walking is easy, although the initial section of track to the north of the station is frequently wet and boggy. Beyond the lodge, path conditions are dependent on the weather. While the route is easy enough to navigate, the going is soft and prone to squelching in places. It rises up through a narrow opening in the glen before descending to the riverbank.

Staoineag is a simple dwelling, a tin-roofed cottage with two wood-panelled rooms and a sleeping loft in the attic. There are a few basic items of furniture and open fireplaces in each of the main rooms.

Above the bothy stands the ruin of another structure, probably outbuildings and, up until at least the 1970s there was a small corrugated iron shed next to the bothy. The concrete base is all that remains of this.

Home originally to a shepherd and his family, a hermit called Ken Smith occupied it more recently. Known amongst bothygoers as Ken o'the Staoineag, he came to the area from Derbyshire and later moved to a log cabin constructed in woodland on the western side of Loch Treig. Christened 'Ken's Holt', he brewed his own wine and made occasional forays into Fort William for supplies.

SITE STATS

GRID REF	NN 296678	OS LANDRANGER	41
		OS EXPLORER	385
WALK IN	7km		
HOW TO GET THERE		Walk in from Corrour Station via Creaguaineach Lodge, following track signed for Fort William	
NEAREST REFRESHMENTS		Licensed café/restaurant at Corrour Station House (7km)	
NEAREST ACCOMMODATION		Corrour Station House (7km) or Loch Ossian SYHA (9km)	
NEARBY BOTHIES		Staoineag (NN 296678)	

CORROUR OLD LODGE, RANNOCH MOOR

Numerous potential pitches are to be found in and around the ruins of what was once Scotland's highest shooting lodge. Built in the 19th century, the lodge sits at an elevation of 540 metres above sea level and commands excellent views across the bleak expanse of Rannoch Moor.

With the opening of the West Highland Line over the moor, a more accessible lodge, designed by Frank College of Wharr & College, Glasgow, was built at the eastern end of Loch Ossian in 1896. The former shooting lodge is believed to have served briefly as an isolation hospital or sanatorium in the early 20th century before the roof was removed in the 1930s and it fell into ruin.

From the old lodge, the enormous scale of Rannoch Moor comes sharply into focus. It is a vast plain of brown grass and heather, liberally sprinkled with lichen and moss-encrusted boulders. Small lochans dot a landscape where rivers and streams run riot.

The moor, which covers 50 square miles, is framed by a series of mountain ranges that funnel it west towards Glen Coe, east to Loch

Rannoch and south to the Black Mount. During the Ice Age, it was covered by an extensive ice cap, glaciers radiating out across the west central Highlands.

After the ice melted, water remained, the gentle slope, slow drainage and high rainfall carpeting the underlying granite with blanket bog. Until Roman times it was partially wooded but today the moor is virtually treeless, save for small copses on loch islands and the famous Rannoch Rowan, which clings precariously to a boulder by the A82.

SITE STATS

GRID REF	NN 407647	OS LANDRANGER	41
		OS EXPLORER	385
WALK IN	7km		
HOW TO GET THERE		Walk or cycle the Road to the Isles track north from Rannoch Station or south from Corrour Station, both on the West Highland Line.	
NEAREST REFRESHMENTS		Tea room at Rannoch Station (11km), licensed café/restaurant at Corrour Station House (7km)	
NEAREST ACCOMMODATION		Moor of Rannoch Hotel, Rannoch Station (11km), Corrour Station House (7km) or Loch Ossian SYHA (5km)	
NEARBY BOTHIES		None	

LUBNACLACH, RANNOCH MOOR

An oasis of flat grass in the rough wilderness of Rannoch Moor, the land around the ruined cottage at Lubnaclach (also frequently referred to as Luibnaclach) is excellent for camping. This isolated former estate keeper's cottage sits close to the West Highland Line and was occupied until the 1970s.

The West Highland Line was one of the last significant railway projects to be undertaken in Scotland. Construction began on October 23, 1889, and the line opened to passengers on August 7, 1894.

It was an ambitious undertaking, the route between Glasgow and Fort William crossing varied and challenging terrain. One of the most difficult tasks facing the engineers was how to lay tracks over waterlogged Rannoch Moor. After numerous failed attempts, which threatened to bankrupt the whole project, they eventually hit upon the ingenious idea of floating the line across the moor on a blanket of tree roots, brushwood and thousands of tons of earth and ash. Much to the delight of the company accountants, it worked.

The North British Railway absorbed the West Highland Line in December 1908 and the company was in turn absorbed into the London and North Eastern Railway in 1923.

Upon nationalisation, the line became part of the British Railways network and after miraculously escaping the cuts of Dr Richard Beeching in the mid-1960s it remains one of the most scenic railway journeys in Europe.

To the west of Lubnaclach an old right of way ran through the glen, descending to Kinlochleven. It was well used by navvies working on the construction of the West Highland Line. However part of the route was lost when the Blackwater Reservoir was created.

Today the cottage is a shell of a building with no roof but the sturdy walls afford some shelter from the elements for cooking while nearby streams offer a steady flow of water.

SITE STATS

GRID REF	NN 373643	OS LANDRANGER	41
		OS EXPLORER	385
WALK IN	4.5km		
HOW TO GET THERE		Walk in from Corrour Station via Loch Ossian Youth Hostel	
NEAREST REFRESHMENTS		Licensed café/restaurant at Corrour Station House (4.5km)	
NEAREST ACCOMMODATION		Corrour Station House (4.5km) or Loch Ossian SYHA (3km)	
NEARBY BOTHIES		None	

RUIGH-AITEACHAIN, GLEN FESHIE

Glen Feshie is a traditional Scottish glen, flanked by craggy mountains, dotted with Scots Pine trees and home to wandering herds of red deer.

One of the best places to camp is by Ruigh-aiteachain bothy. There are plenty of flat grassy pitches amongst the pines and the bothy is always open, should you need to retreat from the elements to the comfort of a roaring log fire.

It is not easy to pinpoint Ruigh-aiteachain's precise history in the colonisation of the glen but a survey of huts and shielings undertaken in 1682 recorded a shieling at 'Rieattachan'. It was not, however, until the early 19th century that the site was more comprehensively developed.

In 1825 the estate was leased to the Duke and Duchess of Bedford for the shooting season. The family built a lodge at Ruigh Fionntaig, on the west side of the river and, across the water, the Duchess established a lodge of sorts at Ruigh-aiteachain in 1830.

Known as the Duchess of Bedford's Huts, a tiny rural idyll of fairy-tale cottages sprang up. Built of wood and turf and topped with thatch they offered the Duchess and her guests a secret paradise where they could enjoy the country life.

A regular guest was the artist Sir Edwin Landseer. In his day the most popular painter in Britain, he discovered the Scottish Highlands in 1824 and, despite having the pick of the estates, Glenfeshie became his favourite.

One of his most famous legacies in the glen was a deer fresco painted on the chimney breast of one of the huts. He watched, studied and sketched red deer for what was to become his most famous painting of a stag, the Monarch of the Glen. As the building deteriorated, a timber structure was erected to protect the murals, at the request of Queen Victoria, who visited in 1860.

At Ruigh-aiteachain there remains the bothy and the remnants of three other buildings, one of which has a prominent chimney stalk. The 1st Edition OS survey of 1869 recorded nine buildings set in two groups. Contemporary accounts, paintings and early photographs confirm the south group of buildings as the Duchess of Bedford's Huts. After her death in 1853, the huts fell into ruin.

The hut containing Landseer's frescoes was enclosed within a wooden hall and this apparently served as a church during the early part of the 20th century. However, very little of the artwork survived the ravages of time and in 1954 a falling tree destroyed this, the last of the huts. The chimney stack, however, remains.

It is unlikely that Ruigh-aiteachain was one of the Duchess of Bedford's Huts, although it was certainly located in the same general area. While her structures were all rather temporary in nature, the bothy is a robust stone building that has survived rather better.

SITE STATS

GRID REF	NN 847928	OS LANDRANGER	43
		OS EXPLORER	384
WALK IN	4.5km		
HOW TO GET THERE		Walk or cycle in from the road end at Auchlean, a short drive south of Kincraig via Feshiebridge	
NEAREST REFRESHMENTS		Suie Hotel, Kincraig (15km)	
NEAREST ACCOMMODATION		Hotels, B&Bs and hostel in and around Kincraig (15km)	
NEARBY BOTHIES		Ruigh-aiteachain (NN 847928)	

WHITE BRIDGE, GLEN DEE

White Bridge is a great meeting place of routes, an interchange point of rights of way emerging from wild and mountainous country. To the north lies the Lairig Ghru, one of Scotland's most famous passes. Glen Tilt heads south, leading walkers through the hills to Blair Atholl. Follow the Geldie Burn west for Glen Feshie or go east through Glen Dee to Linn of Dee and Braemar.

If you plan to call a halt to proceedings here, the best pitches are a little way up Glen Dee where there are some spectacular waterfalls and pools on the River Dee. Alternatively, head south for 2km to find flat grassy ground by Ruighe Ealasaid, also known as Red House, close to the Geldie Burn.

Currently an empty shell of a building, Ruighe Ealasaid, was built in the early 19th century to house a shepherd and his family. Following land clearances, it was remodelled as a gamekeeper's cottage but was abandoned in the first half of the 20th century and was used as a bothy until it deteriorated to the point where it was no longer habitable or safe.

In 2000 work was undertaken to repair and stabilise the structure and, after a lengthy period of uncertainty over its future, it has now been adopted by the Mountain Bothies Association and will be renovated as an open bothy with completion due in 2020.

SITE STATS

GRID REF	NO 018884	OS LANDRANGER	43
		OS EXPLORER	OL57
WALK IN	4.5km		
HOW TO GET THERE		Walk or cycle west on track from Linn of Dee	
NEAREST REFRESHMENTS		Fife Arms Hotel, Braemar (14km)	
NEAREST ACCOMMODATION		Hotels, B&Bs and SYHA hostel in Braemar (14km)	
NEARBY BOTHIES		Corrour (NN 981 958)	

FALLS OF TARF, GLEN TILT

There is a fine linear walk to be had through Glen Tilt, from Blair Atholl, in the south, to Braemar, in the north. Along the way, the route passes remote Falls of Tarf, a spectacular waterfall at the convergence of the Tarf Water and River Tilt. The Bedford Bridge, a bouncy little suspension bridge, carries the path over the water below the tumbling cascade and close by, on either side of the river, there are some great spots for wild camping.

Continue north through the glen and equally good pitches can be found by the ruins of Bynack Lodge and by the Geldie Water.

Glen Tilt is one of the great historical rights of way in Scotland, and there is little doubt that the legal battle to establish its status in 1849 did more than any other event to raise awareness of the importance of fighting to maintain rights of way.

The Scottish Rights of Way & Access Society was formed in 1845 when access to the countryside was often made difficult by Victorian landowners. From its Edinburgh beginnings, the society quickly became national in response to issues further afield, the most significant case of the time being Glen Tilt.

In 1847 John Balfour, a supporter of the society and professor of botany at Edinburgh University, led a group from Braemar through Glen Tilt. Heading south, the party met the Duke of Atholl and his men who promptly blocked their way. An acrimonious encounter ensued and it only ended when Balfour and his students climbed over a wall and ran off down the valley.

The society took the duke to court and, after lengthy legal proceedings, the route through Glen Tilt was officially proclaimed a public right of way.

SITE STATS

GRID REF	NN 983795	OS LANDRANGER	43
		OS EXPLORER	OL51
WALK IN	21km		
HOW TO GET THERE		Follow tracks and paths north from Blair Atholl through Glen Tilt	
NEAREST REFRESHMENTS		Blair Atholl (21km)	
NEAREST ACCOMMODATION		Hotels, B&Bs and campsite in Blair Atholl (21km)	
NEARBY BOTHIES		Tarf Hotel (NN 927789)	

DERRY LODGE, GLEN DERRY

Sitting at the convergence of three glens – Glen Derry, Glen Lui and Glen Luibeg – and on the junction of a trio of tracks offering access to the mountains of the Cairngorms, the flat grassy plains around Derry Lodge have long been popular with campers and backpackers.

Sheltered by the remnants of Scotland's ancient Caledonian Forest, this riverside location is well placed for hikes on to the high peaks and there are plenty of Munros to choose from, including Scotland's second highest peak, Ben Macdui. If you don't fancy the mountains, there are miles of low level rights of way to explore, including the famous Lairig Ghru pass which links Coylumbridge, near Aviemore, with Braemar.

Derry Lodge is now a shadow of its former self, a dilapidated shell of a building that is desperately in need of some care and attention. There is no access to the lodge and, as such, it offers no refuge from the elements.

There has been a building on this site since the 18th century. The initial structure was a simple cottage. In the early 19th century this was extended to create a small hunting lodge. Later the earlier L-shaped building was enlarged to form a U-shaped plan. This phase of development saw a heightening of the west gable to accommodate an attic floor with dormer windows and an east wing was added.

The building has close connections to the Dukes of Fife and the Royal family. King Edward VII was a frequent visitor and stayed at the lodge on numerous occasions.

In the early 20th century, modern conveniences were added in the form of a toilet on the ground floor and a bathroom upstairs. However, by 1955 the estate no longer required the lodge and it passed to the Cairngorm Club. A new passage and scullery were added. In time, however, the club left the lodge and it remains to this day unoccupied.

Over the years there have been various plans for the structure, one of which would have seen it renovated into accommodation for hillwalkers. Another proposed its demolition. Owned by the National Trust for Scotland, the Category C listed building is currently on the Buildings at Risk Register for Scotland.

SITE STATS

GRID REF	NO 041934	OS LANDRANGER	43
		OS EXPLORER	OL57
WALK IN	5km		
HOW TO GET THERE		From car park at Linn of Dee, follow path and track north through Glen Lui	
NEAREST REFRESHMENTS		Fife Arms Hotel, Braemar (16km)	
NEAREST ACCOMMODATION		Hotels, B&Bs and SYHA hostel in Braemar (16km)	
NEARBY BOTHIES		Bob Scott's Bothy (NO 042932)	

ALTANOUR LODGE, GLEN EY

After an agreeable morning blasting anything that moved off the moor, what better way was there to relax and unwind than over a bite of lunch and a dram or two of whisky snug in the confines of a remote lodge in one of the wildest glens in the Eastern Highlands?

The Victorians certainly concurred and so they built Altanour Lodge at the head of Glen Ey. It served their needs well for many a hunting season, offering refuge from the often hostile elements with the bonus of a roaring log fire.

Sadly its days were numbered. Although stalking continued, the advent of the Land Rover sounded the death knell for such sanctuaries and, abandoned by the sporting elite, the solid stone structure slowly succumbed to the elements.

All is not lost, however, as the crumbling edifice offers an historical heart to a cracking wild campsite, confirming the Victorian's knew location was all-important as they devoured the Scottish countryside. Altanour is a real rough country hideaway.

Protected by swaying stands of spruce and larch and flanked by a horseshoe of lofty mountain peaks, the lodge is still open for overnight visitors, although the absence of a roof, and most of the walls, means all guests must bring a tent.

Despite its seclusion, Altanour is remarkably accessible. From the tiny hamlet of Inverey – a stone's throw Mar Lodge – a track leads all the way to the long lost front door.

The route follows Glen Ey south, staying close to the Ey Burn. Two kilometres from Inverey, the stream tumbles through a rocky gorge, known as The Colonel's Bed. Legend has it that John Farquharson of Inverey, a man known as the 'Black Colonel' due to his violent temper, hid here from the forces of law and order after he was outlawed in 1666 for the murder a Ballater laird. He took refuge on a rocky ledge deep in the chasm, his lover Annie Ban visiting daily with parcels of food.

A bed he may have found, but a peaceful night's sleep would definitely have eluded him. The gorge is a raucous, noisy place, a constant flow of boisterous white water carousing smooth rock before dropping headlong into deep, inky pools. A precarious path, signed from the track, leads down to a viewpoint, but great care is needed when exploring this striking spot.

As the track heads up the glen, the grasp of civilisation becomes increasingly tenuous. Occasional ruins point to past habitation but aside from the track and a couple of bridges, there is really nothing in Glen Ey other than the landscape and the nature that fills it, and that really is its draw.

As the route swings round the eastern flank of Creag an Lochain, crossing the stream, the isolation really hits you. You are on your own now, with only the mountains for company. Up ahead Carn Bhac, Beinn Iutharn Mhor and An Socach, conspire to create a seemingly impenetrable head wall, the heathery slopes dotted with rough, uninviting rock and scree.

Altanour Lodge soon makes its presence known, thanks to those spruce and larch trees. On arrival, the best pitches are to be found on the east side of the lodge, between the track and the trees, or on the flat grass between the trees and the river where a low wall affords shelter.

SITE STATS

GRID REF	NO 082823	OS LANDRANGER	43
		OS EXPLORER	OL52
WALK IN	8km		
HOW TO GET THERE		From Inverey, walk or cycle up Glen Ey	
NEAREST REFRESHMENTS		Fife Arms Hotel, Braemar (15km)	
NEAREST ACCOMMODATION		Hotels, B&Bs and SYHA hostel in Braemar (15km)	
NEARBY BOTHIES		None	

LOCH CHON, TRINAFOUR

Loch Con lies to the north of the much larger Loch Errochty reservoir, the pair separated by the rounded mound of Sron Chon. While there are plenty of grassy pitches on the banks of Loch Errochty, its smaller neighbour feels wilder and more remote.

The walk in is just over 4km along a good track that branches west off one of the hairpins on the minor road rising north from Trinafour. Usefully, for those planning to venture this way and perhaps explore the surrounding hills, stalking contact information tends to be posted on the gate at the start of the track during the season. There is no parking by the gate but space may be found just up the road by Maud Loch

The track leads to a wee bothy perched at the eastern end of Loch Con. With one window overlooking the water, it is more a lunch hut than a bothy, although the visitors' book suggests it is not uncommon for folk to spend the night here.

Inside there is bench seating, a couple of tables and, set into the stone gable, a fireplace. Outside there is room enough to pitch tents on the flat grass around the building.

However, explore a little further along the northern shoreline and there are some delightful, sheltered spots on a wooded promontory, beyond stone ruins.

SITE STATS

GRID REF	NN 688679	OS LANDRANGER	42
		OS EXPLORER	OL49
WALK IN	4km		
HOW TO GET THERE		From minor road, walk or cycle track to fishing hut	
NEAREST REFRESHMENTS		Struan Inn, Calvine (14km)	
NEAREST ACCOMMODATION		Struan Inn, Calvine (14km)	
NEARBY BOTHIES		Loch Chon Fishing Hut (NN 694679)	

LOCH NAN EUN, GLEN SHEE

Loch nan Eun is a high level loch (787m above sea level) lying below the peaks of Beinn Iutharn Mhor and Glas Tulaichean. It is a wild and remote spot and, in good weather, a tranquil place to pitch a tent.

Five Munros lie within easy reach of the loch – Glas Tulaichean, Carn an Righ, Beinn Iutharn Mhor, An Socach and Carn Bhac.

Access is via a 10m track walk from Glenshee Parish Church, by the old military road bridge in Spittal of Glenshee, through Gleann Taitneach which, beyond sheep grazing land and Dalmunzie Castle, offers some good riverside pitches of its own.

SITE STATS

GRID REF	NO 063778	OS LANDRANGER	43
		OS EXPLORER	OL52
WALK IN	10km		
HOW TO GET THERE		Follow track north from Spittal of Glenshee through Gleann Taitneach	
NEAREST REFRESHMENTS		Café at Gulabin Lodge, Spittal of Glenshee (10km)	
NEAREST ACCOMMODATION		Gulabin Lodge, Spittal of Glenshee (10km)	
NEARBY BOTHIES		None	

LOCHAN OISINNEACH MOR, DUNKELD

A rich mix of woodland, rolling moor and craggy wee hills, the countryside to the north of Dunkeld is dotted with small lochs and reservoirs, linked by a network of tracks popular with walkers and mountain bikers.

Lochan Oisinneach Mor is one of the furthest out from the Perthshire village and, as such, tends to attract fewer visits than its neighbours, making it a quieter spot to pitch up.

While much of the shoreline is either too rocky or too heathery to contemplate putting up a tent, by the outflow, where the track from Dunkeld via Loch Ordie, arrives at the loch, there is scope to strike camp on small patches of grass dotted with evergreens.

There are two main routes in. The first begins at Cally Car Park (NO 023437), to the north of Dunkeld, and follows a well-walked track to Mill Dam and then on to Loch Ordie, via Raor Lodge. From the northern tip of Loch Ordie, a track progresses north via a ruined cottage to Lochan Oisinneach Mor.

The second starts in Ballinluig and follows a minor road towards Milton of Tulliemet. Branch on to a track signed for the loch and continue up past Tulliemet House and a steading at Blaranrash and track then path continue over pasture and moorland to the loch.

SITE STATS

GRID REF	NO 027546	OS LANDRANGER	43
		OS EXPLORER	379

WALK IN   8km

HOW TO GET THERE   Follow tracks north from Dunkeld or minor road then tracks east from Ballinluig via Tulliemet

NEAREST REFRESHMENTS   Ballinluig (8km) or Dunkeld (9km)

NEAREST ACCOMMODATION   Ballinluig (8km) or Dunkeld (9km)

NEARBY BOTHIES   Sarah's Bothy (NO 037541)

GLEN DOLL

The best pitches in Glen Doll are to be found beyond Glendoll Forest, above the tree-line. Here, below craggy peaks and rocky bluffs, the valley has a wild and secluded atmosphere. The walk in is straightforward. Set off from Glen Doll Ranger Base and follow Jock's Road west, passing below Glendoll Lodge.

Built in the 19th century as a shooting lodge by Lord Southesk, it was for decades a popular youth hostel, sadly closing in 2002.

Jock's Road is well signed. The route is named after John (Jock) Winter, one of a number of local shepherds who, in 1887, joined forces with the Scottish Rights of Way & Access Society to challenge a landowner who intent on denying them access.

After a lengthy legal battle that ended in the House of Lords in 1888, the old road was established as a right of way, setting a precedent that has protected public access to scores of other routes in the Scottish hills.

The route follows the tumbling White Water upstream, swapping a solid forest road for a much more pleasant track that eventually emerges into open countryside beyond the northern fringes of the forest. Here flat grassy pitches are to be found alongside the river.

Glen Doll has long been bereft of a formal campsite. There was one adjacent to the car park but, thanks to some rather rowdy campers and a few too many boozy parties, it closed down. In a bid to fill the void, the ranger service has designated three short stay wild camping sites. They are located in Glendoll Forest (NO 252766), in a former quarry above Acharn (NO 280764), and by the River South Esk, south of Moulzie (NO 285768).

SITE STATS

GRID REF	NO 246768	OS LANDRANGER	44
		OS EXPLORER	379

WALK IN	4km
HOW TO GET THERE	Follow Jock's Road from Glen Doll Ranger Base through Glendoll Forest
NEAREST REFRESHMENTS	Glen Clova Hotel (9km)
NEAREST ACCOMMODATION	Glen Clova Hotel (9km)
NEARBY BOTHIES	Davy's Bourach (NO 232778)

GLEN MARK

Striking north from the western end of the Glen Esk road, Glen Mark is a well-walked valley. However, the majority of visitors venture only as far as Queen's Well, an ornate fountain constructed to commemorate a visit by Queen Victoria in 1861, or pass through en route to Scotland's most easterly Munro, Mount Keen. Bear west at Queen's Well, however, and there is wilder terrain to explore.

A track and then footpath follow the Water of Mark upstream through this twisting vale. Beyond the convergence of the Water of Mark and Burn of Doune a flat grassy plain offers ample scope for camping.

Continue further up the glen and a rocky gorge peppered with deep pools offers wonderful opportunities for wild swimming.

Higher still, seek out Balnamoon's Cave, the clandestine hiding place of a fleeing Jacobite. The cave guards its secrets well. Countless visitors have sought out its sanctuary and seclusion. Most have returned disappointed, unable to locate the spot amid the craggy cliffs and rock-strewn slopes. And therein lies its beauty for the concealed location really was a matter of life or death for rebel laird James Carnegy, the 6th Earl of Balnamoon, as he fled the blood-soaked battlefields of Culloden.

The Argyll Highlanders were sent to rout him out and, after a year in hiding, Carnegy was captured and taken to London for trial. Following confusion over his identity he was pardoned and released in 1748.

To locate the cave, hike up the glen and, above the first waterfall encountered, the path emerges from heather moor on to a flat plain of grass, located below a second, higher fall. Bear left to find a narrow path that rises through the heather and rocks to the cave entrance, a slender slit barely discernible from the chaotic jumble of boulders.

SITE STATS

GRID REF	NO 399834	OS LANDRANGER	44
		OS EXPLORER	OL53/OL54

WALK IN	6km
HOW TO GET THERE	From Invermark, at the end of the Glen Esk road, follow track through Glen Mark to Queen's Well then head west, following Water of Mark upstream
NEAREST REFRESHMENTS	Panmure Arms Hotel (30km)
NEAREST ACCOMMODATION	Hotels and B&Bs in Edzell (30km)
NEARBY BOTHIES	Shielin of Mark (NO 337827)

AUCHINTAPLE LOCH, GLEN ISLA

Auchintaple Loch, with its quaint wee boathouse and wooded promontory, is a real hidden gem. It has long been a favourite with anglers, but few walkers ventured this way until the arrival of the Cateran Trail, a long-distance trail which runs close by.

For wild campers, the wooded promontory, on the east side of the water, is the spot to head for, offering sheltered pitches below old Scots pine and larch trees, all boasting fine views across the loch.

Auchintaple is an artificial loch, created in 1884 for fishing and, with trout the main catch, continues to prove popular with anglers who pay good money to potter about on the water. And, on a sunny day, who could blame them.

The hike in starts in Glen Isla, just south of the bridge over the River Isla at Little Forter. There is a small layby capable of accommodating a couple of cars, next to a Cateran Trail information board.

Go through the high gate and head up the track. It is quite a strenuous pull but there are views back over Mount Blair and Forter Castle should you need an excuse to pause from time to time.

The route rises to a junction where the Cateran Trail continues ahead. Stay on the main track as it sweeps right, leading directly to the boatshed. Continue round the southern shoreline, passing through two high gates. Beyond the second of these a path leads on round the shoreline, crossing the embankment dam to reach the promontory.

SITE STATS

GRID REF	NO 197646	OS LANDRANGER	44
		OS EXPLORER	OL53

WALK IN	2km
HOW TO GET THERE	A short track walk leaving the Glen Isla road just south of the bridge at Little Forter
NEAREST REFRESHMENTS	Glenisla Hotel (8km)
NEAREST ACCOMMODATION	Glenisla Hotel (8km)
NEARBY BOTHIES	None

CARLINGHEUGH BAY, ARBROATH

A short hike north from Arbroath's Victoria Park via a well-walked coastal trail, Carlingheugh Bay's wide sweep lies between headlands of rugged sandstone.

Passing through the Seaton Nature Reserve – where black headed gulls, shags and guillemots may be spotted on the rocks – the route climbs steadily to the Needle's E'e, a narrow hole worn into the soft sandstone by the sea, before curving inland to Dickmont's Den, a deep gash in the coastline.

These geological quirks may be impressive, but they have nothing on the Deil's Heid. This sturdy sea stack forms a wonderfully evil face that glares down at the lapping tide.

The sandstone cliffs part to reveal Carlingheugh Bay, a wide cove with a sliver of white sand breaking up the rocky foreshore. At the far end there are two caves, accessible when the tide is out. One tunnels through the headland, emerging into a concealed inlet beyond. While the beach itself is rocky, there are long swathes of grass to pitch on.

SITE STATS

GRID REF	NO 669424	OS LANDRANGER	54
		OS EXPLORER	382

WALK IN	2.5km
HOW TO GET THERE	Follow the clifftop path north from Whiting Ness, Arbroath, via Dickmont's Den and the Deil's Heid sea stack
NEAREST REFRESHMENTS	Arbroath (3.5km)
NEAREST ACCOMMODATION	Hotels and B&Bs in Arbroath (3.5km)
NEARBY BOTHIES	None

SIDLAW HILLS, DUNDEE

As the nearest upland area to Dundee, the Sidlaw Hills has a long history of wild camping and bivvying, city folk escaping for a night or two in the great outdoors. Amid the low hills and heathery slopes, there are plenty of sheltered grassy spots among scattered copses of larch and pine.

To the north of the summit of Scotston Hill, where a swathe of heather moor meets woodland, on the fringe of the forest there are peaceful places to camp close to a simple stone howff.

When last visited in the Spring of 2019, someone had constructed a quaint little stone fireplace complete with spit, stool and a whittled wine bottle while others have left stumps of wood to sit on.

Access on foot is either from the Balkello Community Woodland Car Park (NO 365385), on the minor road between Kirkton of Auchterhouse to Tealing, or from Kirkton of Auchterhouse (NO 346389).

Join the track (signed Denoon) climbing north over the western side of Auchterhouse Hill. Follow it over its high point, where there is a gate and stile, and descend to a waymarked junction. Continue down to cross a stream then go left, crossing a stile, and follow the burn upstream.

SITE STATS

GRID REF	NO 350406	OS LANDRANGER	54
		OS EXPLORER	380

WALK IN	3.5km
HOW TO GET THERE	Walk in from Balkello Community Woodland Car Park or Kirkton of Auchterhouse
NEAREST REFRESHMENTS	Birkhill (10km)
NEAREST ACCOMMODATION	Dundee (12km)
NEARBY BOTHIES	None

ABOUT THE AUTHOR

James Carron is a freelance writer based in Dundee, Scotland. He specialises in writing about active outdoor pursuits and his passions include hillwalking, backpacking, wilderness adventures and camping.

Connect with me online...

Website: www.jamescarron.com

Email: jimcarron@gmail.com

BOOKS BY JAMES CARRON

BOTHIES, HUTS & HOWFFS IN THE HILLS: PERTHSHIRE & ANGUS

amenta.ink

Bothies are basic shelters in remote corners of the countryside, a home from home in the hills for walkers, backpackers, mountain bikers and others who love spending time in the great outdoors.

Scotland has a long tradition of 'bothying' and, while the better known ones are easily found, one of the great pleasures of exploring the nation's mountains and glens is stumbling upon one for the first time - and finding the door open.

This guide takes some of the guesswork out of the equation, listing unlocked habitable shelters, ranging from comfortable, well-equipped bothies suitable for overnight stays to simple wooden huts and howffs offering protection from the elements, a place to break for lunch or a bolthole in an emergency.

Covering Perthshire and Angus, the fully illustrated guide details the location of each bothy, hut or howff by grid reference, offers advice on how to reach it and outlines what to expect upon arrival.

SECRET SCOTLAND

amenta.ink

Welcome to Scotland... Not to the Scotland of glossy tourist brochures, airbrushed landscape photographs, coach parties, visitor centres and woollen mill cafes, but to a nation of secret, treasured places, free of crowds and tartan trappings.

Here, we veer off the well-trod tourist trail and wander down backroads and byways to reveal the country's unusual and offbeat attractions, quirky curiosities and hidden gems, secluded and less well-known spots that await discovery.

Of the 50 attractions listed in the book, most can be visited at any time of the year, day or night, with no booking required or admission charged.

So, whether you want to wish upon an ancient stone, spend the night in a Royal lodge or hermit's bothy, drive an alpine road, climb a manmade hill, spot gnomes all at sea, descend into a pagan canyon or see where oil rigs go to die, pack a bag and enjoy the journey...

HIGHLAND HERMIT – THE REMARKABLE LIFE OF JAMES MCRORY SMITH

amenta.ink

James McRory Smith lived for over 30 years at Strathchailleach, one of the most remote cottages in the Britain Isles. The building sits alone in a vast tract of empty, featureless terrain to the south of Cape Wrath, in Sutherland. There is no access road, no running water, no electricity and no telephone.

Yet James McRory Smith survived here, battered by the elements and devoid of human company. His story is a fascinating account of a man pitting his wits against the wilderness, enduring endless isolation and existing, for a large part, off the land. James' lifestyle belonged to a bygone age, yet he lived it in the 20th century, turning his back on the luxuries and conveniences of the modern world.

This biography provides readers with an inspiring account of a modern day hermit. It offers a rare insight into an alternative way of life, one that is far removed from the norm.

At a time when people are becoming increasingly concerned about consumption and consumerism, and their impact on the environment, James McRory Smith's story demonstrates the practicalities and challenges of the frugal, self-sufficient lifestyle many people dream of. However, this is not intended simply as a social history, is also a true-life story of adventure and survival.

TIN TABERNACLES AND OTHER CORRUGATED IRON BUILDINGS IN SCOTLAND

amenta.ink

Corrugated iron is a common sight in industrial and agricultural buildings. Less common are the tin tabernacles, mission halls, hospitals, schools, houses and cottages constructed during the 19th and early 20th centuries.

Derided by some, overlooked by others, those that remain standing to this day are legacy to a branch of architecture that dared to be different. Born of necessity, this black sheep of the building trade matured into a distinctive and delightful character of both the rural and urban landscape.

Charting the history of corrugated iron as a construction material from its earliest days in the 1830s through to the Second World War, this book explores the once thriving market for kit-built kirks, ready to assemble reading rooms and off-the-shelf schools that sprung up across Scotland, often in some of the most remote and far flung corners of the country.

Inexpensive to erect and frequently regarded as a temporary fix, many of these quirky little buildings remain standing and in use to this day.

For more information on Amenta Publishing titles, available in both ebook and paperback formats, please visit www.amenta.ink.

Printed in Great Britain
by Amazon